GRIFFIN POETRY PRIZE

Anthology 2025

A SELECTION OF THE SHORTLIST

Edited by ANNE MICHAELS

ANANSI

PAST WINNERS AND SHORTLISTS OF THE GRIFFIN POETRY PRIZE

2001

International
Yehuda Amichai
Translated by Chana Bloch and Chana Kronfeld
Fanny Howe
Les Murray
Paul Celan
Translated by Nikolai Popov and Heather McHugh

Canadian
Ghandl of the Qayahl Llaanas
Translated by Robert Bringhurst
Anne Carson
Don McKay

2002

International
Victor Hernández Cruz
Christopher Logue
Les Murray
Alice Notley

Canadian
Christian Bök
Erín Moure
Karen Solie

2003

International
Kathleen Jamie
Paul Muldoon
Gerald Stern
C. D. Wright

Canadian
Margaret Avison
Dionne Brand
P. K. Page

2004

International
Suji Kwock Kim
David Kirby
August Kleinzahler
Louis Simpson

Canadian
Di Brandt
Leslie Greentree
Anne Simpson

GRIFFIN POETRY PRIZE
Anthology 2025

Published in Canada and the USA in 2025 by House of Anansi Press Inc.
houseofanansi.com

House of Anansi Press is a Global Certified Accessible™ (GCA by Benetech) publisher. The ebook version of this book meets stringent accessibility standards and is available to readers with print disabilities.

29 28 27 26 25 1 2 3 4 5

Cataloguing data available from Library and Archives Canada

Cover design: Kyra Griffin and Chloé Griffin
Cover artwork: *2 Sphinxs* by Leonor Fini © Leonor Fini / ADAGP, Paris / CARCC Ottawa 2025
Interior cover artwork: *Chain*, 2010, by Chloé Griffin
The quotation on the back cover is an excerpt from the poem "Flesh" by Yusef Komunyakaa from the book *The Chameleon Couch*

House of Anansi Press is grateful for the privilege to work on and create from the Traditional Territory of many Nations, including the Anishinabeg, the Wendat, and the Haudenosaunee, as well as the Treaty Lands of the Mississaugas of the Credit.

Canada Council for the Arts Conseil des Arts du Canada
ONTARIO ARTS COUNCIL
CONSEIL DES ARTS DE L'ONTARIO
an Ontario government agency
un organisme du gouvernement de l'Ontario

With the participation of the Government of Canada
Avec la participation du gouvernement du Canada | Canada

We acknowledge for their financial support of our publishing program the Canada Council for the Arts, the Ontario Arts Council, and the Government of Canada.

Printed and bound in Canada

2005

International
Fanny Howe
Michael Symmons Roberts
Matthew Rohrer
Charles Simic

Canadian
Roo Borson
George Bowering
Don McKay

2006

International
Kamau Brathwaite
Durs Grünbein
Translated by Michael Hofmann
Michael Palmer
Dunya Mikhail
Translated by Elizabeth Winslow

Canadian
Phil Hall
Sylvia Legris
Erín Moure

2007

International
Paul Farley
Rodney Jones
Frederick Seidel
Charles Wright

Canadian
Ken Babstock
Don McKay
Priscila Uppal

2008

International
John Ashbery
Elaine Equi
César Vallejo
Translated by Clayton Eshleman
David Harsent

Canadian
Robin Blaser
Nicole Brossard
Translated by Robert Majzels and Erín Moure
David W. McFadden

2009

International
Mick Imlah
Derek Mahon
C. D. Wright
Dean Young

Canadian
Kevin Connolly
Jeramy Dodds
A. F. Moritz

2010

International
John Glenday
Louise Glück
Eiléan Ní Chuilleanáin
Valérie Rouzeau
Translated by Susan Wicks

Canadian
Kate Hall
P. K. Page
Karen Solie

2011

International
Seamus Heaney
Adonis
Translated by Khaled Mattawa
François Jacqmin
Translated by Philip Mosley
Gjertrud Schnackenberg

Canadian
Dionne Brand
Suzanne Buffam
John Steffler

2012

International
David Harsent
Yusef Komunyakaa
Sean O'Brien
Tadeusz Różewicz
Translated by Joanna Trzeciak

Canadian
Ken Babstock
Phil Hall
Jan Zwicky

2013

International
Ghassan Zaqtan
Translated by Fady Joudah
Jennifer Maiden
Alan Shapiro
Brenda Shaughnessy

Canadian
David W. McFadden
James Pollock
Ian Williams

2014

International
Rachael Boast
Brenda Hillman
Carl Phillips
Tomasz Różycki
Translated by Mira Rosenthal

Canadian
Anne Carson
Sue Goyette
Anne Michaels

2015

International
Wang Xiaoni
  Translated by Eleanor Goodman
Wioletta Grzegorzewska
  Translated by Marek Kazmierski
Michael Longley
Spencer Reece

Canadian
Shane Book
Jane Munro
Russell Thornton

2016

International
Norman Dubie
Joy Harjo
Don Paterson
Rowan Ricardo Phillips

Canadian
Ulrikka S. Gernes
  Translated by Per Brask and Patrick Friesen
Liz Howard
Soraya Peerbaye

2017

International
Jane Mead
Abdellatif Laâbi
  Translated by Donald Nicholson-Smith
Alice Oswald
Denise Riley

Canadian
Jordan Abel
Hoa Nguyen
Sandra Ridley

2018

International
Tongo Eisen-Martin
Susan Howe
Layli Long Soldier
Natalie Shapero

Canadian
Billy-Ray Belcourt
Aisha Sasha John
Donato Mancini

2019

International
Raymond Antrobus
Daniel Borzutzky
Kim Hyesoon
Translated by Don Mee Choi
Luljeta Lleshanaku
Translated by Ani Gjika

Canadian
Dionne Brand
Eve Joseph
Sarah Tolmie

2020

International
Abigail Chabitnoy
Sharon Olds
Etel Adnan
Translated by Sarah Riggs
Natalie Scenters-Zapico

Canadian
Chantal Gibson
Doyali Farah Islam
Kaie Kellough

2021

International
Victoria Chang
Valzhyna Mort
Srikanth Reddy
Yi Lei
Translated by Tracy K. Smith and Changtai Bi

Canadian
Joseph Dandurand
Canisia Lubrin
Yusuf Saadi

2022

International
Gemma Gorga
Translated by Sharon Dolin
Douglas Kearney
Natalka Bilotserkivets
Translated by Ali Kinsella and Dzvinia Orlowsky
Ed Roberson

Canadian
David Bradford
Liz Howard
Tolu Oloruntoba

Between 2001 and 2022, the Griffin Poetry Prize was awarded in two categories—Canadian and International—with the total number of submissions received split approximately 50/50. In 2023, the prizes were combined into one major prize to emphasize the international nature of poetry, transcending all borders and languages.

2023

Iman Mersal
Translated by Robyn Creswell
Ada Limón
Susan Musgrave
Roger Reeves
Ocean Vuong

2024

Halyna Kruk
Translated by Amelia M. Glaser and Yuliya Ilchuk
Jorie Graham
Ishion Hutchinson
Ann Lauterbach
Homero Aridjis
Translated by George McWhirter

PAST RECIPIENTS OF THE GRIFFIN TRUST FOR EXCELLENCE IN POETRY LIFETIME RECOGNITION AWARD

Robin Blaser (2006)
Tomas Tranströmer (2007)
Ko Un (2008)
Hans Magnus Enzensberger (2009)
Adrienne Rich (2010)
Yves Bonnefoy (2011)
Seamus Heaney (2012)
Adélia Prado (2014)
Derek Walcott (2015)
Adam Zagajewski (2016)
Frank Bidart (2017)
Ana Blandiana (2018)
Nicole Brossard (2019)
Yusef Komunyakaa (2021)
Fanny Howe (2023)
Don McKay (2024)

PAST WINNERS OF THE CANADIAN FIRST BOOK PRIZE

Emily Riddle (2023)
Maggie Burton (2024)

CONTENTS

PREFACE

Poetry is an exactitude: in its desire, in its seeking, in its doubt. In its grief, its provocation, its praise. Whispering, deafening, intimate, a harrowing, a balm, an inebriation, a gratitude, a seduction, a rallying cry, a message left for the others. An almost inaudible abstraction or a blasting idea, a suggestion, an investigation, a plea, a trace. A poem that is alive never leaves us behind, always takes us with it, into its cry, its wound, its peace, into these times, this place, this present moment. This irrefutability. In its singularity it speaks to all. The poem thinks and breathes; every line, every syllable, in its tension, torsion, duration, music, is an instruction for breathing; here, now; alive together.

It has been a privilege to read the 578 submissions to the 2025 Griffin Poetry Prize, and to be immersed in this work alongside my fellow judges, Tomasz Różycki and Nick Laird. The experience of reading over the course of the year was deeply moving; and the experience of reading alongside Tomasz and Nick, knowing their openness and attentiveness, the incisiveness, acuity, and respect with which they were engaged, was its own hope: the engagement of a reader is a quiet recalibration of the world; in that intimacy, both writer and reader listening, there is possibility—of witness, of justice, of something mended. Not alone.

Every poet situates us in the world in their own way. Tomaž Šalamun's language ignites and reignites its own internal chain reactions, feedback loops, and adrenaline; it collides with itself, breaks open, juxtaposes—a brain and heart fully firing and on fire, then suddenly at rest, in wonder, in grief, in gratitude. Šalamun has written:

"I could touch my brain directly / with my tongue"; "language is 'articulated' and 'mute' / at the same time." The dead "crackle"; "shrapnel / gets in your salad"; "I didn't stop / writing. Only now, when / I raise a glass of water." This is the chaos of being alive and the chaos of history—of nations invaded, split apart, systematically deconstructed and reconstructed, where speaking the wrong dialect or a metaphor could cost you your life. As Šalamun is quoted in the introduction to *Kiss the Eyes of Peace*, translated by Brian Henry: "One has to be very precise not to be corrupt or used" (p. xviii). But what compels in Šalamun's language is not that it disconnects, but rather that it coheres in its own way, or perhaps more accurately, in the way of the world: these poems map the incoherent world. Šalamun writes: "I was fighting to be free within my writing. And just this was subversive, and therefore political" (p. xviii); "to be free within your writing, this is also the center of the real responsibility of the world" (p. xix).

Nicolás Guillén is also, as his translator Aaron Coleman describes him in his introduction, "a maker and breaker of forms" (p. vii). Guillén's *The Great Zoo* is not just an animal zoo, or even a zoo where humans are also acknowledged as animals; its taxonomy also includes objects, ideas, processes—myth, geology, astronomy, seas and winds, clouds and stars, guitars and gangsters, beetles and mountain ranges. Guillén has collected the wild, fierce, ugly, dreaming, scheming, murderous, lonely; its specimens include the meteorological and metaphoric. In this way, his zoo is without confinement, or rather its confinement is so universal and ubiquitous that it contains everything. As the poem ends, we pass by the Exit sign, which is, of course, ironic—because it is impossible to exit the great zoo, from which we are inextricable. We are embedded, complicit in everything we see and know, make and unmake, enslave and destroy, corrupt and confine, even the largest forces of nature. The tamer himself is part of the collection. Guillén's whimsy is also deadly serious; like the tiger "captive in its own cage / of hard black stripes," we live within the horrors of history, dictatorship, and species extinction, all of our own making. Reading Guillén, we cannot help but ask ourselves how we would describe and categorize what's around us, every experience, object, creature; every injustice and ideal; and how we—both cager and caged, tamer and tamed—would describe ourselves.

Durs Grünbein's poems inhabit intimately both the personal and the historical, masterfully seamless as the non-orientable surface of a Möbius loop. In *Psyche Running*, translated by Karen Leeder, poems superimpose past and present as if they were a single event, a single place, a single day—which they are: memory is always a present moment, inextricable, complicated, complicit. We stand in history, history stands in us, simultaneous; mirror and reflection, a single voice split, speaking in unison. And in that historical inseparability, Grünbein is also naming something else—central, fundamental, deeply moving: "Because every life goes off track in its own way." He writes, "The metronome / of hours stops dead and we're in—the eternal glyptotheque. / Taking the taxi again, past all the crumbling arcades, / past capitals truncated by time … / That one day shrank, as we touched, to a single hour— / And we sank, in each other's arms, into the hotel mirror."

In *Modern Poetry*, Diane Seuss—with everything at stake—interrogates the value of poetry, asking if and how poetry matters—does it know, does it prove, does it rescue, does it abandon … Why should we turn to it, in the face of injustice, insecurity, powerlessness, class inequity, betrayal, abandonment, every form of love, rapture, rupture, desire, doubt, despair … Seuss challenges her assumptions so that, in the end, whatever remains can be trusted. And she challenges herself in the most inescapable way: *Modern Poetry* is argued through the act of writing poems, so that the ineffable must, in the end, be given its due. These poems—moving, acutely aware and self-aware, agile, with an edge of humour—move through the book's argument to its final line, with its powerful, unassailable conclusion.

Carl Phillips's *Scattered Snows, to the North* contains a deep tenderness, made even more profound by uncompromising acuity. These poems know that there is nothing blurred or indefinite in tenderness—it does not soften, it specifies. The precision in these poems—not only in astonishingly articulated ideas but perhaps especially in their uncertainties, doubts, seeking—is piercing. Acceptance, understanding, or even the sudden, correct, impossible question, can depend on a single moment as well as "the mind's insistence," in the marshes, in the forest, in the smell of rain. We accept, or we don't, what is beyond understanding; we love or we don't, in spite of or because of the limits that define us and the "competing / powers of revelation and distortion."

These poets face mortality, memory, surrender, persistence, dispossession, brutality, every form of love and grief. They do not turn away from what is bitterly or beautifully unanswerable. In their profound looking, they give us courage to look too. Not alone.

GRIFFIN POETRY PRIZE
Anthology 2025

KAREN LEEDER

TRANSLATED FROM THE GERMAN WRITTEN BY DURS GRÜNBEIN

Psyche Running

Durs Grünbein's *Psyche Running* is a brilliant overview and selection of a poet who satisfies our hunger to be serious, as again and again he finds himself "between words and things." Karen Leeder's adept translations establish a new version of Grünbein in English: universal, lyrical, philosophical.

23 August 1939

An unremarkable day,
one of the last summer days of peace time.
For those strolling in the Tiergarten, tourists
on Unter den Linden, visiting the Reich capital,
Berlin, caught in the grip of propaganda,
for the sweethearts in the Sparrow Hills,
Mandelstam's favourite place, high above Moscow,
this day would scarcely mean a thing.

Fly back to the beginning, my soul, back
to the years of formation, years of illusion
for millions, back to the eerie threshold,
where the dragons almost kissed, like the
towering pavilions at the Paris World Fair,
and the *Polyp Cosmocrator*, harbinger of destruction,
fell as a shadow over the masses.
Do your rounds through peacetime Europe
before the massacres began, the purges
in the paranoia-terrain of the new workers' paradise,
the labour camps, construction sites, steelworks
in the second the world trembled, when anything was possible
between Fascism and Communism,
the psychotic division of the world into left and right.
As the bearded vulture circles in the Swiss Alps,
imagine the 'world of yesterday' still whole and undestroyed.

It was an unremarkable day, when a few
squat men, inferior characters, tyrants,
exchanged whole peoples between them,
when the blind leading the blind of the century
decided to hold their peoples as hostages,
to play with borders, with landscapes.
The hour of the cartographers in their offices,
the hour of the massing of files (Soviet state security, Gestapo),

registration of all people in their own state
as in all occupied zones
with identification numbers, photos, fingerprints
for continued use (work or death).

Dive down to the depths of time, the shallows of time,
just look at them, the peoples then, choked
by politics, cheated of a League of Nations.
Of peace, work, their own deaths,
as the havoc began.
Just look at them, the chances, the love stories
that came to nothing, the conferences
(Rapallo, Locarno, finally Evian),
when the weak were bartered away,
and no one wanted them: the boat was full.

Think back to the day, a summer's day,
the last time people in the cities of Europe
would sit in their cafés unwatched,
almost unsuspecting, laughing and chatting
with the frantic gestures, the shy glances
of figures in the fast-forward of archival footage,
the blue haze of their cigarettes above the pavement.
Think of the Surrealists' picnic, the grown-up games
on the shores of the Côte d'Azur,
this ultimate summer of avant-gardes,
the great, the retarding moment
before, on the Spanish border,
the last of the humanists
died wretchedly in a dry riverbed.

18

Elbe-valley, seven bridges, you can see them in your dreams.
Bet you can trace the city's every contour in your sleep?
Like Polyphemus in his cave once knew his sheep.
Like the astronomer loves his favourite constellation,
from Hellerau to Cotta you know every property.
The blindfold kid will always find the penguins in Dresden zoo.
They say good luck lives on in families. Well, misfortune too.
Shut your eyes and ruins are the first thing you see
burnt into your retina, even after forty years.
Familiar as the lines upon your hand, the city map appears.

Mimosa

Sometimes at night it comes back, that one day in Rome,
when the snowstorm at the centre of the globe abates,
your fingers glide south and mine.
                                                            The metronome
of hours stops dead and we're in—the eternal glyptotheque.
Taking the taxi again, past all the crumbling arcades,
past capitals truncated by time, torsos flayed by the sun,
sneaking in behind the backs of those dripping-wet naiads
before plunging at last into Bernini's fantastical world.
Take it all in! Gazelles in short skirts and skin-tight trousers,
a patchwork of marble, elephants carrying obelisks.
Baroque flights of clouds, drunk here in espresso cups.
Stopped at the traffic lights, street boys flogging mimosa.
That one day shrank, as we touched, to a single hour—
And we sank, in each other's arms, into the hotel mirror.

Island without Sirens

for Alexander Kluge

And suddenly you saw it, far below
the coast road, after the twelfth curve,
stomach surging from the hair-pin drive.
En route for the south; so we sped on
perched above the drop, windows down.
Sorrento with its villas, its fan palms,
had been swallowed by the plug-hole
of the mirror in a great green swirl.
It hung in the haze, a hulk of bare rock.

The sea, dead still. Not a trace of myth,
but for the yachts decked out in chrome
glinting in the sunlight. On a white hull
we made out 'Nausicaa' in faded letters.
How the rumour started, I don't know—
but someone said this was it, so we parked up
in the middle of nowhere, on the open road.
High above, an orange grove aflame,
and below us, out in the blue, the island.

It was disappointingly bare. In the scree
of limestone baked hard by the sun
not even a twig left for the cormorants.
And the silence stretched for miles,
making one think of test-sites, dead craters,
the acoustics of bombed-out opera houses.
Those fat spectral birds with the long necks,
the singer in the grand finale with his top C,
they had all flown—and what remained
was moon rock absorbing every echo.

Interior with Owl II

The owl: one eye fixed on you, as you
go about your business in the gloom,
your shiny, outlandish face.

She scans you, reads your thoughts
before you think them—and, know this,
no idiocy escapes her.

She followed you from your schoolbook.
Across oceans and distant lands. Through
the years, her gaze on the back of your neck.

How human her face in the light,
as she lowers her heavy lids
slowly from top to bottom.
The other way round only in sleep,
like all birds, all reptiles.

The owl: you never saw her fly
in the gloaming, as they say.
She was always there in the mirror.

Sat there looking right through you
with those huge, binocular eyes,
like the spirits of the dead that are so alive.

Hypothesis

Where does it come from and where does it go:
the boulevard of the eleven thousand poems
that are written every day (on average)?
That roaring interchange, exchange, of words: see
how we speed from place to place since Apollinaire—
just a short step from Isfahan to the Antilles.

They exist because in verse one flies as swift as thought.
Because every life goes off track in its own way,
and every cry is lost in the blue of the sky.
We are speech-walkers, caught up in the polylog,
and could not really say which epoch is ours,
when sleep tears the body away.
Just that it is myths that drive history on
and many a poem could one day save a life.

AARON COLEMAN

TRANSLATED FROM THE SPANISH WRITTEN BY NICOLÁS GUILLÉN

The Great Zoo

The Great Zoo by Nicolás Guillén is one of the masterpieces of Latin American poetry. Originally published in Spanish in 1967 and translated by Aaron Coleman with a subtle understanding of the contexts of colonial oppression and exoticism, this bilingual edition remains a relevant commentary on our times. *The Great Zoo* seeks to integrate history, society, nature, and dreams into the territories of this singular park. It is not only an atypical bestiary of nonsensical and imprecatory zoography, not only a humorous book of fables with strange morals, but also a surprising essay of social criticism that mocks the taxonomic and classificatory pride of man pretending to gather, in cages, the living complexity of nature. The zoo's fauna comprises ideas, emotions, phenomena, anthropomorphized animals, and men who are animals; the descriptions of the species are masterpieces of suggestion, working on our imagination with great force. The book, entertaining and moving, is simply beautiful.

Hurricane

A thoroughbred hurricane,
just arrived in Cuba from the Bahamas.
Raised in Bermuda
but has family in Barbados.
Has been to Puerto Rico.
Ripped out the mainmast of Jamaica by the roots.
Was going to ravage Guadeloupe.
Did ravage Martinique.
Age: two days.

Moon

Metal mammal. Nocturnal.

You can see
its face eaten by acne.

Sputniks and sonnets.

Lynch

Lynch from Alabama.
Tailpiece in the form of a whip
and three-pointed hooves.
Tends to appear
with a great cross in flames.
Feeds on Black people, ropes,
fire, blood, nails,
tar.

Captured
close to a hanging. Male.
Castrated.

Tonton Macoute

For René Depestre

Canid,
abundant in Haiti during the Era
of the Quadruped.
                                        Model specimen
found in the presidential corral
just next to the ruined
wilderness of the palace.
(Port-au-Prince.)

Lost its left paw to a bullet
in front of the Champ de Mars
in a popular uprising.

It will die in a few short days
due to the machete wound
sunken in its forehead.

They're now preparing its display case
in the Museum of Natural History.

The Clouds

The Cloud Sanctuary.
Capacity: 84 clouds.
A new experience, because there are
clouds from sunup to sundown
and from many different countries.
(Management forecasts more.)

Lanky-tongued like a bird,
reddish,
the daybreak clouds,
made by the farmer's brief dreams
and hollow dawns.
Restrained,
made of dry and firm cotton,
the motherly, immovable noonday ones.
Like serpents in flames,
the ones that announce the Evening Star.
A curiosity: there are some from Uganda,
driven by winds from the great Lake Victoria.
Some from El Turquino, lying low.
Some from the Maritime Alps.
Some from Pico Bolívar.
Black, with heavy breasts,
those of the storm.

Romantic clouds too,
like, for example, those that fog up
the sky of love. The rosy-colored ones
from sixty years ago
in the Christmas cards.
Clouds with angels.
Clouds the shapes of titans,
of well-known maps *(England)*,

of kangaroos, lions.
In brief, a respectable load.

However,
these *Polar* breeds, extremely rare,
there was no way to bring them back alive.
They arrived in brine, express
from Greenland, Norway, Newfoundland.
(Management has promised
to exhibit them behind glass for the public.)

Guitar

They went out hunting for guitars,
underneath the full moon.
And they brought back her:
pale, fine, lithe,
ceaseless *mulata* eyes,
a waist of open wood.
She's young, just barely flies.
But already she sings
when she hears, in other cages,
the flittering wings of *sones* and *coplas*.
His somber*sones* and her lonely*coplas*.
On her cage is this inscription:
"Caution: she dreams."

CARL PHILLIPS

Scattered Snows, to the North

It is Carl Phillips's mastery that these poems measure, weigh, question, prevaricate: "it seemed," "maybe," "what if," "it's hard, these days, to know for sure what's true," "We weren't afraid. Nor / unafraid." And it is Phillips's magic that this diction renders greater precision, not less; an astonishing accuracy in naming the liminal space from which our comprehension, acceptance, farewells, memories emerge and submerge again. Phillips has found a way to articulate love in all its assertions and disguises—calibrated in all its doubt, tenderness, forms of desire, loyalty, solitudes. In the poem "Stop Shaking," he writes: "I keep making the same avoidable / few mistakes that I've always made, and then regretting them, / and then regretting them less." In tone and diction, these poems never stray across the line between honesty and privacy. How grateful the reader is to enter and re-enter these poems, to be entered by them. For in their articulation of what is most elusive—what we cannot understand and also somehow know—in their recognition of unanswerable human limitation, is a kind of forgiveness.

Regime

As I took off
my clothes, I
watched him taking

his own off. The sound
of rain was for
once not the sound

of wind shaking
the rain steadily loose
from a stand

of river birch. It's hard
to believe in them,
the beautiful colors

of extinction; but
these are the colors.

Like So

From attention to adoration
is a smallish distance—

and yet no arrow, no boat
with sail

can cross it

like the mind's insistence.

We'd reached the marshes, by then, that
all the dead must come to. I could see my face,
tilted there, like a solar eclipse viewed indirectly, which
is the proper way, in a basin of water. You must hold it steady,
keep the basin safe from the wind's reach, its competing
powers of revelation and distortion.

Searchlights

All at once, the tiger lilies were out and we'd come too far, world
versus what I've called the world versus what I've made of it
and shaped to my taste, favoring, instead of the sky's edgeless
statement about vastness, the sea's mixed set of questions whose
only answers, finally, are the questions themselves, Is pleasure
in fact a lens to make suffering

more legible, for example, Do
betrayal and loyalty share the same mechanism? In my experience
there's not that much difference, usually, between asking and
to have said quite enough. Sometimes a wind demolishes the trees
that were planted, years ago, for stopping the wind, one had come
to rely on them as upon memory, as when we call
our memories proportionate, even remotely, to what was true,
when all we can really say, or maybe should, is This is what
feels true, mostly, when I think of it now,

his face a brokenness
but as a Paleolithic fragment of a reindeer antler decorated
with an image of a horse might, too, be considered a brokenness,
him turning away from then back towards me, I can see my face,
my mouth moving inside it, I can see the words, though I can't
hear them, finding shape first, then meaning, the way smoke does,
Don't, which is not a question; then just the smell of rain, which is.

Somewhere It's Still Summer

            Here's where they stopped to rest, presumably, this
easy-enough-to-miss depression in the low-cut grass. I like
to think they had a chance to sleep a bit, before
    everything else, all the rest that followed, that they neither
        deserved nor didn't,
        the way I see it. I prefer a clean view—
            always have—unencumbered by moral valence; if given
        paper and told to draw morality, I'd draw a cloud
        of meadowlarks when all at once, as if on some cue long ago
    agreed upon,
they disassemble. If most people would draw
a different picture—or say it *can't* be drawn, morality,
    being abstract, as if that meant shapeless (define shape)—
        that doesn't make me wrong or miles ahead of everyone, it
        means I'm not
            someone else, a fact in which I take no little
        pride, though I try to do so humbly, which is to say, in private,
        I keep my best to myself; my worst
    also. I think the truth
lies elsewhere. As with sex, or the weather, or betrayal,
would you rather be surprised, disturbed, bewitched,
    or merely entertained, is maybe
        one way of putting it. Another:
        they were men who faltered in front of danger the way
            most men do, who haven't had to live with it. The kind
        of men who, having ridden bareback for the first time,
        think they know what it
    feels like, to be a centaur—
the horse's body, the man's
steep chest, all hybridity
    and power, two powers
        especially, lust and intellect, a combination that has
        mostly worked, though we all make mistakes. Right? We
            all do? I know a centaur

when I see. These

were men, riding horses. Absolutely nothing mythological about them.

Surfers

Probably this morning's surfers
aren't that much different from the ones I used to watch
nearly fifty years ago, whose glamour seemed
so much more fixed, more absolute from a distance
than when they got
too close, which is the fault
not of myth, but of turning people *into* myth. I was
a kid then; and they were, more or less, men,
soon they'd be men for real, meaning,
more or less, boys. They rarely
smiled at me. They never
touched me. They mostly pretended not to notice me,
though one time, watching them from where I'd
hidden in a stretch of dune grass, I could see
a couple of them with hands raised to their eyes,
scanning the dunes as if searching, and I stood up,
un-hid myself,
and I could tell they'd missed me. Toward
nightfall, I'm a lighthouse, I'm a lighthouse, I'd sing
to myself but very softly, because boys
aren't lighthouses, that's nonsense, repeat
after me. I could never have guessed at it back then, this
second life. It was all I could do, just to be patient
as they paddled their boards out again, into the waves,
then they'd catch one,
and flashing my arms—extended
in front of me like the twin beams of light that,
softly, they'd always been also—I'd guide the men in:
to shore, then closer, as if there were a choice that summer
—or ever—and I'd chosen, and I could almost still see it, from here.

Rehearsal

By then the point of the forest was the getting through it.
Then it lay behind them, all but its sharper details—flies licking at
dried blood, I think, on a random tree stump—getting swiftly lost,
its muffled birdsong, too, that had come less, it seemed, from
the trees than from beneath, mostly, as if somewhere deep,
deep inside the earth. Maybe meeting you has been
the one good reason I lasted so long in a world that must
eventually not include me, I almost said to him. Past the forest,

the shore, where the land ended, where briefly the waves hitting it
seemed the latest example of how squandering momentum can
become routine; while, upon the waves, the taken-for-grantedness
of shadow play seemed its own example: how one way to prove power
can be to quietly assume it. Then except for offshore, where the dark lay
like—defiantly—a ship at anchor, everything was itself. As it always
had been. They took off their shoes, their clothes.
They swam out to the dark ship.

BRIAN HENRY

TRANSLATED FROM THE SLOVENIAN WRITTEN BY TOMAŽ ŠALAMUN

Kiss the Eyes of Peace

Kiss the Eyes of Peace is an extraordinary English selection of poems from the entire body of work of one of the best Central European poets of the twentieth century, Slovenian poet Tomaž Šalamun, presented by poet Brian Henry with precision and power. The English reader experiences this poetry at its finest, with its characteristic post-Dada, unlimited freedom, and a peculiar and unmistakable lightness of diction. Šalamun turns our reading habits upside down—he creates avant-garde linguistic structures in which the poem hangs on the question, on the collision of the concrete and the surrealistic, where a dance of imagination begins. A hypnotic sequence of extremely condensed phrases makes Šalamun's absurdism a realistic portrayal of a contemporary world where strangeness can be a source of extraordinary beauty. This selection restores faith in the glory and power of poetry, in its wild freedom and beauty.

Quietly Changing

You can inflate a mass murderer's legs
so that they'll be round as balloons, but he won't

notice. This is also the only way you'll track
him down. But where to get a pump? Where to get

a mass murderer? Mass murderers are
safely hidden around salons. If they steer

a cart up a hill, their facial muscles
tremble. I remember a mass murderer at

the camp in Visoko when I was fourteen.
He arranged cans of milk

on a small wooden cart. We talked.
He was from the village. On the left stood

a rectangular hayrack, and because darkness
was already falling, I didn't look him in the eyes.

Painted Desert

When we arrived at the Painted Desert
in Arizona, I remembered Heidegger.
I said to Maruška: I want to go naked
in this sun through the desert,
I remembered that fearful film
by Antonioni, but I was still tempted
to be naked in the sand. Maruška
said: moron! Do you think that I'm going
to watch you vanish at the horizon
and then pursue you with the car
across this sand.
No, I said, we'll both go.
What will happen with Ana, Maruška said.
We'll leave her in the car and give her
cookie. Cookie was at that time
still a drink for Ana. But the desert
will tempt us and we'll never
return, Maruška said.
It's really dangerous, I said, but
your maternal instinct will prevail
and soon you'll come rushing back to Ana.
We had rented a 1972 Chevrolet Impala
with such strong air conditioning that we could
keep the temperature at 60° Fahrenheit.
Chase me through the sand with the Impala.
Too dangerous, Maruška said, but
I opened the door and started
to tear off my clothes because
I remembered Heidegger and Ed Dorn,
who has been living on cocaine now for three years.
All his relationships were relationships
with junkies. Ack! How hot and dizzy
the sand was! The desert is
a fantastic orgasm, more intense than

a woman. Ana grinned madly and
the sky was nearly black, black air.
The Painted Desert is pink, which is why
it has that name, but if you stand on the sand,
the sand isn't pink, it's just diabolical.
If you lie down on the sand, the sand is
diabolical
God knows if I know I act through codes.
It flashed through me and I remembered
that once, when I still lived with Braco
in those rooms in Gradišče,
I pretended I was Gregor Samsa with such
monstrous peace and sobriety
so much of the time that Braco turned
paler and paler, I asked for
a salad and we went together down the street
because Braco thought it would
sober me up, but I kept
stopping passersby and saying
I was Gregor Samsa and I wanted
a salad, so Braco became
quite ashenly pastel and
convinced that I had gone crazy,
and really, if he hadn't hit me in the head
with his fist in front of the nuns' church
so that I became dizzy and
furious, God knows if I would have come down
at all, and then Braco started vomiting
and I knew he really loved me.
I didn't know that all this could go
so far. I jumped back into the car.
Maruška was just like bronze,
and Ana, who Was starting to perceive
in her little head that this wasn't
funny, was wailing. Maruška was

entirely composed, only her body
trembled, and she calmly
drove the car like some hearse
thirty miles south on Route
66 and stopped at a gas
station. With her hands attached to
the steering wheel, she said get dressed, and I
got dressed and I knew:
she is certainly not a witch, she's fond
of you, you fool, one day this
exhibitionism will tear you apart.
Then we spent five days
in the Grand Canyon, calm and gentle,
and I constantly photographed
Maruška, so the most beautiful
photographs are from America, when Maruška
is standing on the edge of the Grand Canyon
in that beige crocheted dress
we bought on Stari Trg, and I
bought her a Hopi bracelet and a Hopi
ring, Ana plenty of ice cream.

Sonnet of Motion

Stories that have a first scene, a second
scene, a first border, a second border, surrender like
a lump of meat. The brain slips and smacks its lips.
Radical light is always muscular,
it eliminates situations where you can look back.
And from its head leaps another material,
untouchable thoughts. And the swift chamois that
crouches mid-leap, ledges that
consume consciousness and stay
far behind, restraining their scent and
terror—musk. Is the chamois gone, where's
the chamois? He stood a meter, like a notion
of whiteness. Don't search here because
I've spoken. There's consistently nothing here.

Folk Song

Every true poet is a monster.
He destroys the voice and the people.
His singing builds the technology that destroys
the earth so that the worms don't eat us.
A drunkard sells his coat.
A scoundrel sells his mother.
Only a poet sells his soul
to separate it from the body that he loves.

Kiss the Eyes of Peace

Kiss the eyes of Peace, which should spill over
the trees. The sun shines outside and no longer roars
so intolerably. The soul hopes to feel its ribs,
its juice again. The cold agreed with me. If
the wind blows and I walk and look at cars, life
returns me to myself. It would be most
terrible because I'd recognize no one when leaving.
They would be too far away to touch or feel.
I wouldn't keep the memory of love in the black
darkness. A crust of ice forms over boiling lava.
Gradually, I might be able to slide again. Walk
along dusty roads. Shake off my jacket if it's
dusty. There was too much honey and grace, that's
all. A person explodes from too much luxury.

To Read: To Love

When I read you, I float. Like a teddy bear with paws
you shove me into bliss. You lie on me, whom you
demolished. At death I grew fond of you, first among
the born. In a single moment I became your bonfire.

I'm as safe as I've ever been. You are the ultimate
feeling of satisfaction: to know where yearning is from.
I'm in you as in a soft grave. You carve and ignite
all the layers. Time catches fire and vanishes, I hear hymns

when I look at you. You are stern and demanding, tangible. And
I cannot speak. I know that I yearn for you, hard gray
steel. I'd give everything for one touch from you. Look, the late sun

bangs into the walls of the courtyard in Urbino. I died for you.
I sense you and want you. You torment me. Uproot and cauterize me,
forever. And into the spaces you've destroyed, paradise flows.

DIANE SEUSS

Modern Poetry

Diane Seuss's *Modern Poetry* is the culmination of a life spent learning the art, of locating "the beauty of drawing near," of "seeing through time"—and her wry, compelling tone and effortless technique end in something very like wisdom. She has become an indispensable poet.

Modern Poetry

It was what I'd been waiting for my whole life,
but I wasn't ready for poetry. I didn't have
the tools. Roethke—
I appreciated the greenhouse poems,

and decades later saw his bed; toilet, upright
piano in that desolate town where he was raised,
not unlike the desolate town where I was raised.
No greenhouse in my town, but the Green Giant

factory, where mushrooms grew on cow shit.
Wallace Stevens—I wrote a paper on "Loneliness
in Jersey City" having no clue
what he meant by "The deer and the dachshund are one,"

and got an A anyway by faking it.
The professor made us read
"Sunday Morning," which struck me
as long. I couldn't focus yet, I was eighteen. A poem

against heaven, he told us. "Is there no change of death
in paradise? / Does ripe fruit never fall?" That I could
understand, having known some plums,
and that icky-sweet smell of a dead mouse in the wall.

Gerard Manley Hopkins—not modern per se,
but my professor said, one of the first modernists,
so what did modern poetry really mean? Maybe
just fucked up, as Hopkins was for sure, and tongue

twistery, and depressed, Jesuit, maybe bipolar.
I stared at his photograph, the long nose and cleft
in his chin, noticed that even in "No worst, there is none"
he had the wherewithal to put in the accent marks

to school us as to how to hear the thing. And WCW,
Williams, my roommate and I called him Billy C. Billygoat—
I knew something of wheelbarrows, old women,
and as I said, plums, but the prof showed us

how complicated it all really was, the whole "no ideas
but in things" thing, the near rhymes,
depends and *chickens* and *red*, again, I was not yet
capable of being smart and wondered if I ever would be,

though I kept getting A's on the papers, maybe
because the professor felt sorry for me, and I'm not
just saying that. The final modern poet was Sylvia Plath—
a woman, blonde, and I didn't trust blondes,

smart, angry, angry at men, I was told, depressed, cheated
on, dead. I imagined her being in Modern Poetry with us,
mopping the floor with us, with her developed
mind, her ooh and ahh sounds, her thesis, "The Magic Mirror,"

on the double in Dostoevsky. I pictured her calling me
a charlatan, like Gaylord did in class the week we studied her.
He called her a charlatan psychopath, and me a charlatan
for sticking up for her. I had to go back

to the dorm and look up *charlatan* in the dictionary.
A fraud, the dictionary said. A quack, which yes, I was,
though so was Gaylord. Who isn't a quack at eighteen?
I wanted to love Sylvia, but to love her would mean

loving someone who would have hated me.
It would be a few years, after I flunked out
of college, until I took a class called Women's Literature
at the public university down the hill with a teacher

named Stephanie, who looked a lot like Françoise Sagan,
teenage author of *Bonjour Tristesse*, but older and with a cap
of gray hair. Margaret Atwood. Toni Morrison. Adrienne Rich.
Charlotte Perkins Gilman. Plath. Sexton. Lorde.

Kate Chopin. Alice Walker. Djuna Barnes. I was beginning
to understand, but barely. To ask a pertinent question
now and then, like where the hell was Langston Hughes
in Modern Poetry? Dickinson, in Nineteenth Century American Lit?

If Hopkins was a modernist, how about Dickinson,
with her weird rhymes and what Galway Kinnell called
her "inner, speech-like, sliding, syncopated rhythm,"
a counterpoint to her iambic lines? A horse straining at the bit

in the direction of free verse. A woman who drove
a motorcycle to Women's Literature, wore a fringed
black leather jacket, and worked at the Kalamazoo airport
in the booth where people pay for parking was shot and killed there

by her ex-boyfriend. From then on, the class became
something else. Stephanie had us over to her house,
a damp place in the woods. She roasted a goat
and served it to us, shredded, on blue plates.

The books had become more, and less, important.
We spoke of them, huddled on the floor by the fire.
I remember most of all the bushel baskets
of apples and grapes for winemaking, drawing fruit flies.

I'm not complaining. It was all more than I deserved.
The goat. The greenhouse. The liberated blonde badass
on her motorcycle. *Sula*. *Surfacing*. "Sunday Morning."
Ripe plums. My education.

Romantic Poetry

Now that the TV is gone and the music
has been hauled away,
it's just me here, and the muffling silence
a spider wraps around a living morsel.
And at times, often, the unbearable.
I bear it, though, just like you.
Long ago, I bore a suitcase filled with books,
bore it far on city streets. To sell, I guess, at some
used books place, one of those doorways down
steps into dankness and darkness. The scent

of mildewed, dog-eared, fingered pages.
The suitcase, big and square and sharp-cornered,
covered in snakeskin, bought at Goodwill
for a dollar, knowing I had some traveling to do,
some lugging, and I was right.
What books I sold I do not know.
Maybe that's where *Modern Poetry* went.
The cover cherry-red and blossom-white.
I can see its spine in my mind's eye,
pointing downward beneath the dank

and the dark to the water tunneling
under the city and making its way to the river.
Poems sliding down the book's spine
into water, the shock of the cold and dank,
down where my uterine lining, my blood
and cast-off ovulations, cast-off fetal
tissue swims, below the city.
The microdead ride modern poems
like swan boats in the park.
From the park to the river to the sea.

I'm thinking now of PJ Harvey and Nick Cave.
Balladeers. Lovers. Vita and Virginia.
Frank O'Hara and Vincent Warren. Somehow,
we ride our lost loves out to sea. Or they ride us.
It doesn't matter. Poet or poem or reader, the same
ectoplasm. The modern, in time, becomes antique,
and the stone faces of the dead convert to symbols,
ripe for smashing. Come to think of it,
symbols are terrible. As the tyrant
shouted to the masses,

part of his brainwashing campaign:
I know it, and you know it too.
I was twenty-three when I sold off
Modern Poetry and sailed to Italy, seeking
Romantic poetry, which was at one time
modern, and found my way to Rome,
and Keats's death room.
His deathbed, a facsimile.
Everything he touched was burned,
to kill what killed him.

I lifted his death mask from its nail,
cradled it, closed my eyes and kissed his lips
until the plaster warmed,
and stained his face
with the lipstick on my lips. Red
as the cover of *Modern Poetry.*
The color of the droplets of arterial blood
he coughed onto his sheets and viewed
by candlelight. Then he knew he was done for.
His death warrant, he called it.

After those many kisses over his face and eyes,
and the reticulated eyelashes,
cold and tangled,
my lips were blossom-white,
my face, chalked. Like I'd caught
something from him,
and I don't just mean consumption,
though my lungs burned for years.
They still burn.
This is the danger of the ecstasy of kissing

the dead or dying poet on the mouth.
The disease you'll catch—well,
it changes you.
The tingle in the spine,
the erotic charge, will be forever married
to poetry's previous incarnations.
It's why marriage itself never worked for me.
I kept wanting to get to the part
where death parts us
and I could find myself again.

Keats made such a compact corpse.
Only five feet tall, shorter than Prince,
and intricately made. Always,
he was working it, working it out,
the meaning of suffering, the world's,
his own, the encounter with beauty,
nearly synonymous with suffering,
how empathy could extinguish him,
and he could set down the suitcase at last,
or finally deliver him to himself, distinct

as the waves in his hair and the bridge
of his nose. How auspicious,
rare, lush,
bizarre, kinky, transcendent,
romantic, to be young, just twenty-three,
and to cradle him
in my arms, as we listened
to the burbling water
of the Fontana della Barcaccia
from the open window.

Little Fugue State

Far have I wandered not knowing
the names of where,
long have I woven this dress
of human hair, here
I have pitched my tent, here and there,
not knowing my name,
or where, not even the color of my hair
nor why
it tangles so, nor where my comb goes,
nor where my brush,
how far I wandered through underbrush,
into onrush,
nor where my body was, nor what it called
itself, nor the nature
of my calling, nor what my scrawling meant,
not that scrawl then,
nor this scrawl here, nor what a self
could be,
nor what a bee could be, nor breath,
nor poetry,
this dog I've walked and walked
to death.

High Romance

And then Keats's ghost found
that he could no longer love
Fanny Brawne. He'd escaped
the body like a love
letter from its envelope, and he'd flown
like a love letter in a windstorm.
He'd seen that the words
formed from ink melted in the rain.
Words, he now knew—and he'd once been
such a devotee—didn't matter,
or didn't matter so much as he'd believed
they mattered. Something mattered, he knew,
but whatever it was he couldn't put
words to it, or he didn't have the heart
to put words to it. He did feel love,
but it was an arrow without a target.
It was diffuse, like an atomized
perfume, or stars as the poor see them,
who cannot afford glasses. He saw
that Fanny, as she was known,
was a concept, just as he had been a concept.
They each inhabited the same amount
of space, like a tablespoon
of butter and a tablespoon of lard.
In a book, they would each occupy
a single page. Their brains, encased
in cranial bones and flesh and heads of hair,
could each rest on a single, silk pillow.
Ideas, he found, don't die. Even notions fly
like cottonwood seeds through the air.
And love had been a notion. He saw
that Fanny, in time, would slip free of herself,
everything does, in time, even roses,
even stones, foothills, fleas, and poems.

Rhyme, he saw, existed on its own behalf.
He could catch it like a bird catches
an air current. From above, he could see
that Fanny was not trifling. Nothing,
from above, is trifling, nor more compelling
than anything else. His love for her, he saw,
had been an invention of the mind.
Only belief could sustain it, but he
could no longer sustain belief. Now
and then he'd try it on again—love—
like a fancy hat he could not afford
and now appeared ludicrously overdesigned.
Once, his ghost managed to look at her again,
through the gauzy curtains that hung
over her bedroom window. His gaze
was too objective to find her beautiful,
but objectivity itself—that was beautiful.

Love Letter

But what can it be if love is a past-
tense event? And what
was love then
according to my brain
and what
is love now and how do I direct it
like a beam with the power
to excise all that is not love? For a time
I believed getting and keeping
love required lace. Procuring lace
and arranging it
on my body in a certain way.
Isn't that funny and/or strange?
I modulated my voice to the northern
region of its register. Reddened
my lips. This was love's drapery
and music and face.
If you've read *Madame Bovary*, if you've read
gothic romance, you know
the denouement of that arc.
When I first read the word *denouement*
out loud, my ex-husband
laughed at my mispronunciation.
I include it here as an illustration
of the fact that love does not conquer
all. Now when I think
of love, it's like focusing too hard
on the mechanisms of blinking or breathing.
You can be blinded or suffocated
by that degree of self-consciousness.
Like a love letter, love seems to me to exist
on a thin plane, a disintegrating page
covered in words scratched
onto the surface with purple disappearing ink

cooked up in a chemistry lab.
I'm sure I've written a love letter here
and there. Something gauche,
a performance designed toward
the specific outcome of eternity.
I read of a feral dog who could only be captured
by putting the soiled blankets of her puppies
in a live trap. This is my metaphor for a love letter.
I own a letter my father wrote my mother
when they were newly in love.
The stationery is smallish and decorated
with a garish deep red rose in aching
bloom. He spends most
of his language's currency bemoaning
his bad spelling. No wonder
she found him charming. For my people
it is the flaw that counts, but not for all
people. Our narrative is an object
lesson in the fact that flawed people
deserve to be loved, at least for a while.
That's the ephemeral part.
I'm much too sturdy now to invest
in the ephemeral. No, I do not own lace
curtains. It's clear we die a hundred times
before we die. The selves
that were gauzy, soft, sweet, capable
of throwing themselves away
on love, died young. They sacrificed
themselves to the long haul.
Picture girls in white nighties jumping
off a cliff into the sea. I want to say,
don't mistake this for cynicism,
but of course, it is cynicism.
Cynicism is a go-to I no longer have
the energy to resist. It's like living

with a vampire. Finally, just get it
over with, bite me. I find it almost
offensive to use the word *love*
in relation to people I actually love.
The word has jumped off
so many cliffs into so many seas.
What can it now signify?
Shall I use the word *affinity*
like J. D. Salinger, not a good
man, put into the mouths
of his child-genius characters? I have
an affinity for my parents. An affinity
for you. I will make sure you are fed
and clothed. I will listen to you
endlessly. I will protect your privacy
even if it means removing myself
from the equation. Do those sound like
wedding vows? Are they indiscriminate?
Well, then, I am indiscriminate.
I am married to the world.
I have worked it all out in front of you.
Isn't that a kind of nakedness?
You have called for a love letter.
This is a love letter.

Romantic Poet

You would not have loved him,
my friend the scholar
decried. He brushed his teeth,
if at all, with salt. He lied,
and rarely washed
his hair. Wiped his ass
with leaves or with his hand.
The top of his head would have barely
reached your tits. His pits
reeked, as did his deathbed.

But the nightingale, I said.

THE POETS

AARON COLEMAN is a poet, translator, educator, and scholar of the African Diaspora. He is the recipient of fellowships from the National Endowment for the Arts, Cave Canem, the Fulbright Program, and the American Literary Translators Association. His debut poetry collection, *Threat Come Close*, was the winner of the Great Lakes Colleges Association New Writers Award, and his chapbook, *St. Trigger*, won the Button Poetry Prize. He is the translator of Afro-Cuban poet Nicolás Guillén's 1967 collection, *The Great Zoo*, selected for the Phoenix Poets series by University of Chicago Press. His poems, essays, and translations have appeared in *The New York Times*, *Boston Review*, *Callaloo*, and *Poetry Magazine*. From Metro Detroit, Coleman has lived and worked with youth in locations including Spain, South Africa, Chicago, St. Louis, and Kalamazoo. He is an assistant professor of English and Comparative Literature in the Helen Zell Writers' Program at the University of Michigan.

NICOLÁS GUILLÉN (1902–1989) was a prolific Cuban poet, journalist, and activist. Born in Camagüey to parents of African and European ancestry, Guillén worked in printing presses and studied law before moving into Havana's literary scene. A virtuosic maker and breaker of forms, Guillén rose to fame by transforming a popular form of Cuban music into poetry that called attention to the experience of Afro-Cuban people, and he continued to interweave his artistic and political commitments as he travelled the world. Guillén received the Lenin Peace Prize, the International Botev Prize, and Cuba's

National Prize for Literature. In 1961, he was named National Poet of Cuba. He authored sixteen poetry collections, including *Motivos de son*, *Sóngoro cosongo*, *West Indies Ltd.*, and *El son entero*. The first English-language anthology of his early work, *Cuba Libre*, was translated by Langston Hughes.

BRIAN HENRY is the translator of Tomaž Šalamun's *Kiss the Eyes of Peace* and *Woods and Chalices*, as well as Aleš Debeljak's *Smugglers*, and six books by Aleš Šteger, most recently *Burning Tongues: New & Selected Poems*. Henry is also the author of *Permanent State*, ten other books of poetry, and the collection of essays *Things Are Completely Simple: Poetry and Translation*. His work has received numerous honours, including two National Endowment for the Arts fellowships, the Alice Fay Di Castagnola Award, a Howard Foundation fellowship, and the Best Translated Book Award. He lives in Richmond, Virginia.

Slovenian poet TOMAŽ ŠALAMUN (1941–2014) was one of Europe's most prominent poets of his generation and was a leader of the Eastern European avant-garde. He was born in Zagreb, Croatia, and raised in Koper, Slovenia. Early in his career he edited the literary magazine *Perspektive* and was briefly jailed on political charges. He studied art history at the University of Ljubljana, where he found poetry suddenly, as a revelation, describing its arrival in a 2004 interview as "stones from the sky." His work has appeared in over seventy journals and magazines internationally, and he has published fifteen poetry collections in English. Šalamun was a member of the Slovenian Academy of Science and Art and lived in Ljubljana, Slovenia, until his death in late 2014.

KAREN LEEDER is a writer, scholar, and translator of contemporary German literature. She has received many accolades for her translations, including the Stephen Spender Prize for *Childhood in the Diorama* by Durs Grünbein, the John Frederick Nims Memorial Prize for Translation for Grünbein's *The Doctrine of Photography*, and the Schlegel-Tieck Prize for Grünbein's *Porcelain: Poem on the Downfall of My City*. Her work has also been recognized with an American PEN/Heim award for her translation of Ulrike Almut Sandig's *Thick of It* and a second Schlegel-Tieck Prize for *All Under One Roof* by Evelyn Schlag, among other honours. Leeder is the Schwarz-Taylor Chair of the German Language and Literature at the University of Oxford. In 2023, she began a three-year Einstein Fellowship at the Free University of Berlin for her project *AfterWords*.

DURS GRÜNBEIN was born in Dresden in 1962, and now lives in Berlin and Rome. Since 2005, he has been a professor of poetics and aesthetics at the Kunstakademie Düsseldorf. One of Germany's most celebrated poets, Grünbein has earned the Georg Büchner Prize, the Friedrich Nietzsche Prize, the Friedrich Hölderlin Prize, the Berlin Literature Prize, the Premio Internazionale di Poesia Pier Paolo Pasolini, the Tranströmer Prize, and, most recently, the Zbigniew Herbert Prize. His poetry and prose have been translated into multiple languages, including Russian, Italian, English, French, Spanish, Swedish, and Japanese. His book *Ashes for Breakfast: Selected Poems*, translated by Michael Hofmann, was shortlisted for the Griffin Poetry Prize in 2006. Several of his works, including *Childhood in the Diorama*, *The Doctrine of Photography*, and *Porcelain: Poem on the Downfall of My City*, have won awards in Karen Leeder's English translations.

CARL PHILLIPS is the author of seventeen books of poetry, most recently *Scattered Snows, to the North*, and *Then the War: And Selected Poems 2007–2020*, which won the Pulitzer Prize. His other honours include the Jackson Poetry Prize, the Aiken Taylor Award for Modern American Poetry, the Kingsley Tufts Award, the *Los Angeles Times* Book Prize, a Lambda Literary Award, the PEN/USA Award for Poetry, and fellowships from the Guggenheim Foundation, the Library of Congress, the American Academy of Arts and Letters, and the Academy of American Poets. His collection *Silverchest* was shortlisted for the Griffin Poetry Prize in 2014. Phillips has also written three prose books, most recently *My Trade Is Mystery:*

Seven Meditations from a Life in Writing, and he has translated the *Philoctetes* of Sophocles. He lives on Cape Cod, in Massachusetts.

DIANE SEUSS is the author of six poetry collections, including *frank: sonnets*, winner of the Pulitzer Prize, the National Book Critics Circle Award, the *Los Angeles Times* Book Prize, and the PEN/Voelcker Award; *Still Life with Two Dead Peacocks and a Girl*, a finalist for the National Book Critics Circle Award and the *Los Angeles Times* Book Prize; and *Four-Legged Girl*, a finalist for the Pulitzer Prize. She received a Guggenheim Fellowship in 2020 and the John Updike Award from the American Academy of Arts and Letters in 2021. Seuss was raised by a single mother in rural Michigan, which she continues to call home.

THE JUDGES

NICK LAIRD was born in Dungannon in County Tyrone in 1975. A poet, novelist, screenwriter, critic, and former lawyer, his awards include the Betty Trask Prize, the Rooney Prize for Irish Literature, the Geoffrey Faber Memorial Prize, a Forward Prize, the Somerset Maugham Award, and a Guggenheim Fellowship. For many years he taught at universities in the USA, including Columbia, Princeton, and NYU, and is now the Seamus Heaney Professor of Poetry at Queen's University, Belfast.

ANNE MICHAELS is a novelist and poet. Her books have been translated into more than fifty languages and have won dozens of international awards, including the Orange Prize, the *Guardian* Fiction Prize, the Lannan Award for Fiction, and the Commonwealth Poetry Prize for the Americas. Among many other honours, she is a Royal Society of Literature International Writer and a Guggenheim Fellow, has received honorary degrees, and has served as Toronto's Poet Laureate. Her novel *Fugitive Pieces* was adapted as a feature film and was chosen as one of the BBC's 100 Novels That Shaped Our World. Her latest novel, *Held*, was shortlisted for the 2024 Booker Prize.

TOMASZ RÓŻYCKI was born in 1970 and is a poet, translator, and essayist. He is the author of several volumes of poetry, including *Hulanki & swawole* (2024), and the prose work *Złodzieje żarówek* (2023). He garnered critical acclaim for the book-length poem *Twelve Stations* and his collection *Colonies*—both of which, in their original Polish and in translation—earned awards such as the Kościelski Prize, the Wisława Szymborska Award, Le Grand Continent Prize, the Samuel Bogumił Linde Prize, the Václav Burian Prize, the Joseph Brodsky Award, and the Northern California Book Award. He has been shortlisted for the Nike Prize, the Griffin Poetry Prize, and the Oxford-Weidenfeld Prize, among others. Różycki was a fellow of the DAAD Artists-in-Berlin Program in 2018, and was awarded a Senate of Berlin Fellowship in 2020.

ACKNOWLEDGEMENTS

The publisher thanks the following for their kind permission to reprint the work contained in this volume:

"23 August 1939," "18," "Mimosa," "Island without Sirens," "Interior with Owl II," and "Hypothesis" from *Psyche Running*, by Durs Grünbein, translated by Karen Leeder, are reprinted by permission of Seagull Books.

"Hurricane," "Moon," "Lynch," "Tonton Macoute," "The Clouds," and "Guitar" from *The Great Zoo* by Nicolás Guillén, translated by Aaron Coleman, are reprinted by permission of University of Chicago Press/Phoenix Poets.

"Regime," "Like So," "Searchlights," "Somewhere It's Still Summer," "Surfers," and "Rehearsal" from *Scattered Snows, to the North* by Carl Phillips are reprinted by permission of Farrar, Straus and Giroux.

"Quietly Changing," "Painted Desert," "Sonnet of Motion," "Folk Song," "Kiss the Eyes of Peace," and "To Read: To Love" from *Kiss the Eyes of Peace* by Tomaž Šalamun, translated by Brian Henry, are reprinted by permission of Milkweed Editions.

"Modern Poetry," "Romantic Poetry," "Little Fugue State," "High Romance," "Love Letter," and "Romantic Poet" from *Modern Poetry* by Diane Seuss are reprinted with permission of Graywolf Press.

GRIFFIN POETRY PRIZE ANTHOLOGY 2025

The best books of poetry published in English are honoured each year with the $130,000 Griffin Poetry Prize, one of the world's most prestigious and richest international literary awards. Since 2001 this annual prize has acted as a tremendous spur to interest in and recognition of poetry, focusing worldwide attention on the formidable talent of poets writing in English and works in translation. And each year the editor of the *Griffin Poetry Prize Anthology* gathers the work of the extraordinary poets shortlisted for the award and introduces us to some of the finest poems in their collections.

This year, editor and prize juror Anne Michaels's selections from the shortlist include poems from Durs Grünbein's *Psyche Running*, translated by Karen Leeder (Seagull Books), Nicolás Guillén's *The Great Zoo*, translated by Aaron Coleman (University of Chicago Press/Phoenix Poets), Carl Phillips's *Scattered Snows, to the North* (Farrar, Straus and Giroux), Tomaž Šalamun's *Kiss the Eyes of Peace*, translated by Brian Henry (Milkweed Editions), and Diane Seuss's *Modern Poetry* (Graywolf Press).

Judges Nick Laird (Northern Ireland), Anne Michaels (Canada), and Tomasz Różycki (Poland) each read 578 books of poetry, including 47 works in translation from 20 different languages, submitted by 219 publishers from 17 countries.